T0194714

# JAMARION
## Beef Patties

by

LaRina A. Seward

AuthorHouse™
1663 Liberty Drive
Bloomington, IN 47403
www.authorhouse.com
Phone: 833-262-8899

Because of the dynamic nature of the Internet, any web addresses or links contained in this book may have changed since publication and may no longer be valid. The views expressed in this work are solely those of the author and do not necessarily reflect the views of the publisher, and the publisher hereby disclaims any responsibility for them.

Any people depicted in stock imagery provided by Getty Images are models, and such images are being used for illustrative purposes only. Certain stock imagery © Getty Images.

This book is printed on acid-free paper.

ISBN: 978-1-6655-5978-2 (sc)
ISBN: 978-1-6655-5977-5 (e)

Library of Congress Control Number: 2022909206

Print information available on the last page.

Published by AuthorHouse  08/24/2022

authorHOUSE®

Deep in the village near Kingston, in a small shack, Reggae music plays. There are 3 men playing the steel drums, entertaining tourists. There are vendors selling a variety of items... "Ya Mon! Come get your Jamaican Fruit Drinks."

Not far away, a young dark-skinned boy named Jamarion Williams lies asleep in bed. The room is filled with homemade Jamaican dolls and collectibles. His mother, Wanda (is a thick woman wearing a sundress and sandals and sporting sister locks) kicks his bed and speaks to him in Jamaican accent, "Get up! It's Saturday. There is work to do!" Jamarion is startled. His dreadlocks swing in the air. His eyes are droopy. He sits up in the bed and rubs his eyes. "Ok mommy". She sits Jamarion's baby brother (Darius) next to him on the bed. The baby jumps on him and plays (tugs) with his dreadlocks. Jamarion got on both hands and knees and allows Darius to jump on his back. The baby rides on his big brothers back and uses Jamarion's dreads as straps. A large green parrot perches in the window. "Hello Repeat", Jamarion says as he places his brother down and walks over to a drawer. The large green birds says, "Hello, hello." He grabs some bird seed and allows the parrot to peck at his hand. In a Jamaican accent he says, "You

3

are very hungry. I must get ready to work." The bird flies off and Jamarion closes the window.

He gleefully gets ready for the day. He sings reggae as he brushes his teeth and washes his face. He gets dressed and puts on his favorite hat. The mother and son pack up lots of ingredients (lard, flour, meat mixture, etc.) and place in a wagon. Jamarion grabs the handle. His mother wraps the baby on her back and the trio heads down a long unpaved road. "Where is daddy?" he asks. "Fishing." He is curious. "Why can't I go with him?" She takes a breath before saying, "Child your daddy is working. That is how he makes his money. Maybe he can take you when he has time." He appears satisfied with her answer. They continue down the long path with Repeat flying nearby.

After traveling on the bumpy road and passing through the impoverished community, they arrive at a small hut near the beach. The sign in front reads "Beef Patties". Jamarion and his family take the goods inside. His mother reaches for some mail and opens the envelope with a butter knife. It reads:

"My name is Wayne Johnson. I understand you own the property at 651 Beach Rd. We represent a buyer who is looking to purchase property in your area. Call us right away to discuss a potential sale. My buyer can buy your property in "as is" condition. No worry about repairs or closing costs to you! If you have interests in selling at a fair price, please call immediately!"

Wayne Johnson
(658) 565-2121

FLOUR

LARD

8

Wanda tosses the letter on the counter. She ties an apron around her neck and waist and starts to make beef patties. She grabs a large bowl, spoon, flour and shortening. Jamarion sits his brother in a wagon and hits the power button on his iPod. Out comes reggae music. Mom and son perform a dance routine for several minutes before preparing beef patties. The duo prepares the food with rhythm as both mother and son place their hands on their hips and wind their bodies (around in a circle) and stretch out their right arms as they move to the right. They do not notice but Repeat is perched in a tree imitating their dance routine. Jamarion grabs an ice cream scooper and scoops out the beef filling onto the dough. Wanda slices the plantains and pours a large bag of rice into a heated pot.

Later that morning, they serve up the beef patties to customers. Jamarion plays with Repeat on the beach before he sees a pretty girl on the beach under a gazebo. She is throwing a beach ball to her friend. Jamarion stands by and watches as the girls run into the water. Jamarion removes his shirt and duplicates what he sees. He dives in and swims but as he comes up for air, the girls had ran off. He lifts his head out of water in disappointment. His dreadlocks fall in his face.

He later finds the young girls are seated on a blanket enjoying some fruit. Jamarion walks over with 2 beef patties. "Would you like a beef patty?" The girls are elated. "Thank you 'Mon" as they quickly grab the patties. "Mi name is Jamarion." They blush. "Well, my name is Charity and her name is Jamay". Jamarion's eyes are wide open, "Jamay…Hi Jamay" he continues," best beef patties in all Jamaica." Jamay grins and says, "Ya mon." "Are you thirsty?" The two girls quickly nod their heads. Jamarion runs off and finds a coconut tree. He climbs the tree easily with his dreads dangling. He looks up and reaches for 2 coconuts. He looks at the girls smiling. He struggles chopping the coconuts and looks at them in some embarrassment, but he delivers the coconuts with a straw. (Reggae song plays)

"SMILE JAMAICA"

**Lyrics**

And I say girl tell me what's your name
And she tell me that her name is Jamaica
And I said smile, girl, smile
Smile for me Jamaica
And I said smile, girl, smile
Ooh Lord, smile for me Jamaica
Never you cry, here am I
I'm here for you Jamaica

**Artists:** Chronixx, Silly Walks Movement
**Album:** Silly Walks Discotheque Presents Honey Pot Riddim
**Released:** 2013

Later on, the sun begins to set into a gorgeous pink fire ball-a serene scene. Wanda receives her last few dollars of the day. She cleans the kitchen and begins to count the total profits. She sits down on a chair and counts the cash. Just then the patriarch (Devon) arrives. He is tired wearing a dingy T shirt and cutoff jeans and old sandals. "Daddy!" Jamarion shouts as he runs into his father's arms. They embrace. Devon walks over to his wife, "Hello honey." He places his hand on Wanda's shoulder. She touches his hand and looks at him. "How are you Devon?" "I am well. How are you?" She is clearly tired. "I am ok." "You look very tired." She looks a bit worried. "Yes, I am tired, but I will be ok. I am worried about this business. We still owe money to the bank for this place." We are not bringing in the profits like before." Devon looks concerned. He rolls his eyes. "It must be that new café that was built last year," says Wanda. Devon scratches his head. "Yea the developers come here to our country close off our beaches and run all of the mom and pop

stores out of business." Just then Wanda shows her husband the letter she received. He reads it and rolls his eyes and places his hand on his head in disbelief. Jamarion has Repeat on his shoulder watching and listening.

The following day, Jamarion is out with his friends. They each have wagons full of homemade jewelry. His friends notice their friend is not the same. "'What's wrong mon?" Jamarion slowly says, "Mi worried about mi parents. They're not making enough money. Mommy is worried about money hungry investors taking all of the customers." "Oh no! Are they gonna close their Beef Patties store?" He replied, "I don't know." They walk past the Jamaican merchants to a popular tourist area and decide to treat themselves to some Jamaican pastry and Caribbean snow cone. As they hand their coins to the merchant each get gizzada. They lick their lips and bite down into the small coconut pie. They all are aware- It is time to

hustle. As they reach the tourist area, the group of boys go in 4 different directions.

Jamarion walks upon a couple who are apparently lost. "Can I help you find your way?" "We are looking for Coconut Café." Jamarion has money on his mind. "I can show you where it is. Mi name is Jamarion. Why don't you put your bags in mi wagon?" They slowly put their back packs and mini suitcases in the wagon. "I know a better place that makes authentic Jamaican food. The best beef patties in all of Jamaica!" "What is the name?" "Beef Patties," he says with a big smile. "Ya mon its only few blocks away." They nod in agreement. "Can I offer you some souvenirs? I have every souvenir-magnets, glasses, necklaces, T Shirts, buttons, spices, incense, maps and posters!" The man and woman look surprised- they thought he would not stop. "We'll take the magnets and necklaces," he interrupts. Jamarion grabs the souvenirs and pockets the dollar bills. He pulls the wagon and they follow. Before

long, they arrive at their destination. "Ok my friends! Here is Beef Patties." It is the best food ever!" They look at each other and grab their items. Jamarion holds out his hand directing the man and woman to Beef Patties. The male gives Jamarion a tip for carrying the bags in the wagon and they wave goodbye. Jamarion runs into the back door. "Hi mommy!" Wanda and Devon are super busy serving up food. She is quickly putting food onto plates and slicing plantains, while her husband is pulling hot trays out of the oven. He says, "We are busy son." Jamarion quietly leaves the café and meets up with his friends.

After a hot day spending time hustling, they discuss the money that has been made. One of them excitedly shouts, "I made $25 mon!" Another friend says," let's go enjoy the river! It's hot." They began going through the village and into green shrubbery until they meet the river. It is a serene scene- gorgeous green trees, tropical birds singing, water streaming. Together they lift a homemade raft (made of bamboo sticks) and climb aboard. Jamarion takes a large bamboo stick and they float down a river. They pass people in inner tubes. Jamarion spots Jamay. He tries to speed up the raft, paddling faster and faster. The boys onboard the homemade raft appear nervous and surprised as they clutch the edges. Jamarion pushing the raft so fast, they rock side to side. The raft hits a rock and dismantles the raft. They plop into the water (luckily, they all can swim). They stare at Jamarion. Their dreadlocks are soaked. He is so ashamed and embarrassed. He just looks at them.

As the sunsets, Jamarion makes it back to Beef Patties. He is tired and is clothes are dirty. As he approaches, he hears the sound of his parents arguing. "We barely made enough to buy food or even put clothes on our back." Jamarion creeps near the backdoor. He sees his mother upset. "We are only receiving maybe half of the profits we used to bring in." Devon puts his hand on his wife's shoulder saying, "It'll be okay dear. Summer is just beginning. There will be more profits once the tourists began coming in." Wanda swiftly responds," No, if they come they will go to the new restaurants those greedy developers built." Devon tries to encourage his wife. "Well, the tourists want authenticity, dear. At least business has picked up a bit. I know we are not seeing the profits like before." Jamarion walks in and helps with his baby brother, offering him a Sippy cup. Both parents turn around. "Jamarion we were starting to worry about you." "Sorry mama" he says, worried about his parents and their business. Jamarion begins to help clean up.

Wanda and Devon also join in and wipe down the counters and wash the dishes. Once the kitchen was cleaned, they all are tired and turn off the lights and lock the door.

The next day as the sunrises, there is a cool wind amongst the island. Jamarion's window is open, and his dingy curtains move with the wind. The birds are chirping and "Repeat" sits upon the window shield. Wanda opens the door and tells Jamarion to get up. Repeat repeats exactly what he hears, "Get up, Get up". Jamarion suddenly opens his eyes. He pulls himself out of bed, yawning and stretching his arms. "Good morning Repeat." He walks over and puts some bird seed in Repeat's bowl. As the large green parrot pecks away, Jamarion goes to the bathroom. He looks at himself in the mirror and begins to wash his face and brush his teeth. He quickly gets dressed and sits down at the table for breakfast. He reaches for a large yellow box on top of the old refrigerator, grabs a bowl and milk. He hears his parents discussing selling the business again.

Before long, they head out again down the long bumpy trail to Beef Patties. Jamarion is concerned. "Mommy why do you want to sell our store?" Wanda keeps her composure. She does not want her son to worry. She reassures him, "Only if we have to son." They continue down the path once again with Repeat nearby. When they arrive at Beef Patties, they continue the usual routine-Wanda opens the window and they dance as the music plays. Mom and son place their hands on their hips and "wind." As Jamarion turns around he stops and stares at Repeat. He is frozen, looking at the large green parrot, which is mimicking their dance routine. Wanda does not notice- she continues dancing and began cooking. Jamarion remains frozen. He is shocked by the parrot's dance moves. He taps on his mother shoulder. She looks down at her son who is pointing at Repeat, but when Wanda looks at the parrot, Repeat had stopped and looked like a normal bird. "Jamarion, stops playing around boy and get to work." Jamarion is still in shock. He day dreams of having a famous

parrot- enjoying a luxurious life-riding in limousine, stepping onto the red carpet, security like the men in black, photographers taking pictures. Just then, his mother shouts," Jamarion! Get to work. Fill these pastries." He snaps out of his dream and sees his mother has laid out many beef patty shells. Jamarion has the ice cream scooper in his hand and slowly begins to place the fillings onto the pastry.

Later that day, another gorgeous sunset begins. A fiery, peach colored round sun appears in the sky. The family is eating dinner at the table. Baby brother Darius is in his highchair slamming the baby rattle. Both parents barely eat their food as they discuss ways to market their business. It appears a light just went off in Wanda's head. "Perhaps we can make a billboard along the main strip?" Devon takes a sip of his drink, "Ok, that sounds good. We can probably advertise on one of the bigger billboards, so more people can see it." Jamarion tugs at his daddy's shirt. "Daddy! Daddy! I saw Repeat dancing today!" Devon smiles at his son, "Oh really". "Yes daddy! He did mi and mommy's

dance with us!" Both parents look at each other and smile, thinking their son is just making the whole thing up. "Can I bring the camera to Beef Patties daddy? Please, please!" Wanda places her hand on Jamarion's shoulder, "We'll see son." The family enjoys some laughter.

The next morning, Jamarion is up very early playing with Repeat. "Repeat, I saw you dancing. Come on let's do it. " He starts to dance but Repeat just sits and watches. Jamarion tries to get Repeat to dance, many times but each time is unsuccessful. Jamarion scratches his head. He turns on some music, but Repeat does not budge. "Tell mi Repeat, I saw you dancing. Why are you not dancing now?" Repeat only gawks. Just then Wanda opens the door. "Jamarion, son come have your breakfast. We must get started early. There is a cruise ship coming in today. We want to serve lots of customers and make money!" Jamarion walks out of the room and sits at the table. "Mommy what if Repeats dances for us today. Maybe all the customers will want to see him." "Enough! Eat your food!"

Moments later, the Williams family is back on the bumpy trail. There are very large cruise ships afar; the sky is pink as the sun rises. Vendors are busy setting up their booths. You can hear reggae music playing as they approach Beef Patties. Repeat perches himself on his usual branch and Jamarion sets up the video. Wanda opens the window and begins preparing the beef patties. Jamarion turns on the music and they began to dance.

However, before they open up, Jamarion shows the video to his mother. Wanda is shocked and happy at what she sees. Jamarion urges her to do their dance upon opening.

Pretty soon, the awesome smell of Jamaican food and reggae music begins to lure the tourists over. Wanda takes a deep breath just as her son hits the play button. They turn up the volume and begin their dance routine. As they work it out, a young boy points at Repeat. "Mommy look at that bird!" Other people in the area take notice. As Jamarion and his mother dances, a crowd begins to form around Beef Patties. The tourists began to pull out their cellular phones and record. Wanda and Jamarion look back and see the crowd and the bird dancing. They continue their routine and begin serving customers.

Days Later the news and other media outlets are in front of Beef Patties. There are many more patrons enjoying the food. Beef Patties is on the front page of the newspaper, magazines and all over social media but most of all Beef Patties is here to stay and becomes a popular tourist attraction.

## About the Author

**La Rina Seward** has a degree in Journalism and is very passionate about writing. She is a successful author that has also wrote a science fiction novel Mission to Mars.

Printed in the United States
by Baker & Taylor Publisher Services